TEXT 2020

HOW TO WIN YOUR CRUSH

BY: FAITH STEPHENS

How to Win

Your Crush?

You saw a guy in a specific place in your school perhaps, or in your neighborhood's grocery store, or in your village park for the first time and when you get home you couldn't forget his face his eyes, his nose or even his poise and how he looks great in his blue polo shirt.

You're thinking how are you going to be able to know his name, when are you going to see him again, and how to be his friend in the first place to start.

It's going to be really so tough for you huh? Especially when he already wins your heart even just in that first glance.

How are you going to approach him when in that first impression you got is, he's snob or he's not that too friendly and you as well are very hesitant to take the first move because you're shy or you don't want yourself to be misunderstood that he might think you're a flirt etc.

Worry no more!

Just follow these simple steps and advice made only just for you. :-)

If you are a typical shy girl who doesn't have that much confidence in the world to have a boyfriend or let's just say who doesn't have a boyfriend ever

since in your life, here are the simplest word of advice you might want to know…

Continue reading…

Girl, first you have to start into yourself …

Try to look into the mirror of what is lacking on you…

See it to yourself what you needed to add on into your looks, your hair your lips, your eyes, your nails, the way you dress the shoes you prefer to wear bags or purse you have, or even your scent of how you smell that is noticeable to other people or the people around you.

Let's start into your hairstyle.

You might want to absolutely have a new look with your dull straight hair.

There are lots of hairstyles to what pretty girls possess on their own these days, like of Taylor Swift hairstyle, or Anne Hathaway, or maybe Katy Perry or Paris Hilton's amazing look.

You even might want to add color into your hair like chest nut brown, burgundy, blonde, or just typical

wine red that will make you look anew shining and bright.

Some gals, prefer waves into their hairstyles like some curls and slash styles of haircuts, that depends

on your face's shape though or your own preference of the look.

Now, let's move on into your eyes….

Are you the type of girl who wears study glasses or do you have astigmatism which makes you really in the need to wear a pair of nerdy glasses?

I'll tell you, if you really want to look pretty and win your crush, you need to find another way around to that!

There are already new trendy ways to wear those nice and attractive contact lenses out in the market, or if you want to go to your own optometrist to consult and get some advice of what contact lenses will suit you, color, design, and style … it's really really worth it girl, I tell you.

Plus, if you like to have your lashes upgraded? You can also go into your closest Lash clinic make an appointment and have that super trendy curly long lashes on you. Just seek any professional advice before doing so.

Not even that! They also have now the pretty eyebrows fixed! It gets detailed and so much to its shape. I swear it will transform you into a celebrity kind of look.

Now let's go into your nose…if you have a pointed nose, you're very lucky girl! Let's celebrate to that! Even though guys nowadays are picky, when they noticed your nose appealing to their eyes, they'll going to like you right away, so go girl! On the other circumstance, if you don't have that pointy nose, don't be sad, you don't need to go into nose lift or surgery if you don't like or if you're scared to do so, make up can fix that, Yes! Contouring the side of the

nose or the nose bridge or use some brush and put lines that are not really revealing, just enough to do a little bit of contour into your nose to make it look pointy or if you have a brow pencil, you can also do that, just draw thin lines into each side of the nose and make sure to wipe a little using your hands to make it even, and there you go! You're now ready to face the world. :-)

We're now all the way to transform you into a better you…

Continue reading…….

So, let's now proceed into your lips.

If you want to have that Angelina Jolie kind of pouty lips, surgery is okay but it's on your own risk, you need to have all the courage to do it, and if you don't want that, there's also another way around, "the Lipstick" Yes, lipstick! There are various colors of pretty nice lipstick, the not so red, pink, and peach are the trendy ones which are not very revealing and vivid...or if you don't like to put on lipstick, then try to use some lip shiner or lip gloss...that'd do to make you stunning. :-)

Next, is the way how you dress up!

Of course, you need to look amazingly charming and neat into the eyes of your crush! All you have to wear is some skirts but not too short like short shorts or really short that is too revealing even your soul has been to see through. Wear some body con dresses with skirts just right slightly above the knees, or some flirty flower knee level skirts, or maybe some good pair of blue jeans that's never out of style these days, or some nude color blouse that is not too much showy... or you might want to wear some body shrink tops and jeggings , or leggings...depends on where you go or the place you're going , it should be proper and firm and nice neat and clean that your crush if he sees you for an instance will automatically get star struck right at you.:-)

Now let's proceed to your foot wear....

Continue reading....

Now, as a girl...of course you want your feet looks attractive and clean.

Wear shoes that is not too boyish and not too awkward like very high heels which is close to 100% turn off if your crush sees you down on the floor when you get out balanced with those heels! There's no way for you to experience the most embarrassing and that unforgettable situation.

A must wear for heels if you really like to wear heels is 3 inches is okay, it's either close or open shoes or sandals that is comfortable to wear.

If it is open toes you need of course to have your pretty noticeable nail polish not too red and of course not very dark color...you may want to include your fingers as well with the light color nail polish to make it even the feet and the hands. :-)

And then now we will highlight into your make up....

Continue reading…….

As a girl, we all have that vanity stuffs in our vanity drawer… we will include our beautiful face to this of course.

Make-up is a must! But not too much…. Because too much could make you look untidy and not so natural. but a slight make up could not cause you harm or any disadvantages. it will make you even prettier and a head turner. So, when your crush is around, you actually need not to say a word but he himself will notice you pretty gorgeous and seemingly he will notice that you're confident of what dress matching to the make-up you would wear.

The right amount of make-up you wear on your face reflects to your personality.

If you wear heavy make ups, they would notice you as not very easy in your lifestyle…

But if you wear slight make up, they or your crush will attract the positive vibes just looking at you.

Because you're showing light aura, smooth and calm as it is being seen in the eyes of your prince charming.

Let's go into your personality approach…….

Continue reading…….

You might as well want to approach your crush in a positive way and good vibes ☺

We all know that your character adds up points and it is really a big turn on into the guys when you're friendly, approachable, bubbly, and has lots of thoughts to share with.

Be the kind of girl who are always appreciative.

A "hey! Nice shirt! (nice cap) or even Nice phone would be a very great approach for both of you to known each other perhaps.

There's nothing wrong when you say something that you are just appreciating a small thing he have.

Your goal is to gain that positive first impression and not being annoying…because as what the older people say, first impression lasts. So, we're trying to

do good impressions here towards the person you really really like.

If he's around, you wouldn't want to miss the chance, to miss the opportunity to get to know him.

Probably you are curios where he lives, where did he go to school, what's his age, what's his favorite sports, what are his hobbies, what he's up to, and of course his Facebook account, Instagram, Twitter, other social media so you can see what are his thing and last his phone number for you to get to know each other really well. :-)

If he's your crush, Girl you need to have the courage to be as friendly as you are.

Be courteous and polite and kind…

Because if you do, I tell you…

It's going to be worth your wait girl ☺

Those guys don't want girls who don't possess those qualities…

They might be looking for a good face yes……but if you're true to yourself of being good polite and obedient, then you are already a winner when you have those qualities mentioned. Even without having a pretty face ….

Even without not dressing pretty….

Even without not looking sexy….

Even without not getting those nails done….

Even without not wearing make-up and pretty shoes and lashes and good shaped brows….

Because a real guy , or a good guy … when they look for a future girlfriend, they would want positive traits, positive outlook in life, that soon in the future will have hundred percent a good life when they found a girl that is independent, God fearing , trust worthy , someone they could rely on in good times and especially in bad times, that will not going to waste their time into negative vibes, they want a girl whose loyal, and has the very nice quality to stay with all throughout the lifetime. So I hope you enjoyed reading...Till we meet again☺

Moving into College

By: Faith Stephens

World's #1 reader friendly Author

Text
2020

Moving into College

About the Author:

My goal is to share my digital hand writing to the world, and make use of the English language into literary skills, I'm one of those authors who wants to make the world a better place.

Faith Stephens

Introduction:

We all may think and ask what's the purpose of life…

Well, you can learn a lot in life when you learn to find out your purpose in this world.

Let me help you how to look all the answers for your question.

Continue reading……….

Life has many sides to view. When God created you and your mom and dad gave life to you, you already have a value instantly into this world.

When you were a baby, you cry and play and give happiness to your whole family.

Your sweet smile are their hopes, your mumble is their stress relief, your sweet smell is their daily courage.

Every day you are growing, every day you learn new things, you learn new words, and you explore your surroundings.

Your parents will never forget the first word you utter, that day you first say Mama and Papa.

Then when you learn how to turn from back to front, when you learn how to crawl day to day, and learn how to stand and walk,

each of those are already the challenges you surpassed when you were still a baby until you grow up….

Continue reading…………

You started to go to school, from preschool, kindergarten and then elementary, your parents are there with you to show that they're there for you...

They teach you how to do chores, how to finish your homework, they teach you how to do stuffs all around the house and outside the house even in the car and grocery store...

They're there for you physically even in their busy days, and when you needed something for school they're there to provide.

Though it's not always perfect as what you may want it to be, you're blessed because you have their support maybe not that much because your parents need to focus on their life as well trying to make money and do their jobs or business, but know that in their heart they're thinking about you too more than they think of themselves.

It's just that some parents may not be too expressive to show their love, but of course as their child they value you more than they do to themselves, you're their own flesh and blood.

Continue reading............

Now, in grade school you'll be on your own, exploring the surroundings, exploring what to learn in school, drawing, reading, writing and trying to find out if you fit in to singing and or dancing program and contests in your school. Then being able to compete with your classmates in the academic

performance you're one of the tops… you making your parents proud. :-)

Continue reading…………………….

Then you proceed into high school, there you find a strange place ever in your life.

Trying to adjust and trying to make everything familiar… the canteen, the school library, the registrars

office, the prayer room, the guidance counselors' room, the gymnasium, the Audio-Visual Room (AVR),

the school church (when you're into a catholic school, the convent, the school Nurse clinic, the Home

economics room, and lastly the Faculty room. :-)

So, the first day of school is not quite a bit interesting but it's more of introducing yourself into everybody in your classroom,

writing all your class schedules and taking down notes of every detail that your class adviser is providing every info on the board.

Then you meet your new friends. new teachers... and you're classroom crush. :-)

Every day, you're inspired to go to school,

and try to participate in the class because you're trying to impress your crush,

but that crush isn't really friendly.

Time have passed, but still he is still not into you he's just passed in front of you without even saying hi or hello... ☹

But that's okay, you tell yourself that it's not about that,

it's about passing all of your grades and making everything good although the subjects seem not pretty easy.

Continue reading…………………….

Every month there are school events and activities in your school,

so, you just won't feel behind or outdated or no progress at all...

You feel so renewed, you feel encouraged, you feel exciting day by day, you feel like there's never ending of new happenings especially when you're into so much participation

of a dance group or singing contests.

You're pretty much of a star and fond of joining beauty and brain contests into your school programs,

you joined into science quiz, quiz bowl,

spelling contests, flag identification,

and so much more to satisfy yourself of being competitive,

to impress your crush, and to receive good appreciation from your loving family,

to make them proud, and to let them know that you are thankful to life. :-)

After the tiring weekday classes, you find time in doing stuffs in your house like cleaning your own room,

doing arts and crafts in your room,

creating something that makes your eyes spark such as writing a poem,

writing a song lyric, doodling, sketching, painting, writing a short story,

practicing guitar chords, playing the flute chords, doing a collage,

making a scrapbook, writing an autograph,

creating these kinds of arts and literary works and being so proud of yourself.

Continue reading..................

The subjects you have are really challenging, you have these top classmates that really excels in Mathematics, English, History, Economics, Music,

Physical Education...but even though they excel to that, still it's up to individual learning and how to apply these learnings into daily living.

High school years is the most unforgettable moments, so cherish every moment while still in High school, you're only there once in your lifetime.

Continue reading………………………

Finally, you Graduate into High school, being an achiever or not what's most important is you surpassed the long school years and with pride that you did it all by glory and strife … you really strive hard with all those homework, quizzes, exams, oral reading, orientation and everything that makes your nerves shakes involuntarily.

Continue reading………………….

Moving into college, when your parents want you to take up the course you love to took up, such as, Engineering, Nursing, Teacher, Medical Technology, Information Technology, Doctor, Pilot, Maritime Seafarers, Agriculturist, Forestry, Dentist, Computer Science, Accounting, Lawyer, and so much more then you decided one course you really like.

When you're living far from the city then you needed to go to college away from home.

You need to pack up some important stuffs and clothes cause the class is going to start soon after you're being enrolled into the University or College you're interested into.

The hardest part of really would want to finish school is this part,

In which you needed to be away and far from your parents, far from your siblings, far from the other members of the family that's close to your heart, but

you really don't have any option but to go ahead and go to college, cause you're doing this not only for

yourself but to your family. It's an advantage if you live into a place where college is just a block away.

There you're already into living into the city, having your own place to stay.

Adjustments is not as easy as what you think it is, but needs extra efforts too and patience.

As you familiarize your daily classes and classrooms, you are dealing with different people too, they're students yes, but they came from different places just like you.

Some may approach you wanting to be your friend, and some ignores.

But the most important is when you're exploring the school premises and its different departments… there's the English Department, Mathematics, Social Science, Physical Education, Government Constitution, and other major subjects which are related to the course you've taken up.

In College, you will going to have different lessons, and the more research.

You need to be tough enough when going to each of your classes, smart enough to answer activity

homework, but these days it is now easier because of technology, the computer is there, the internet is there, it is such a blessing.

These days you it is more advantage that majority of the schools have now online classes, online study modules and online timetables.

Since of the global lockdown because of the pandemic situation, all schools have their new rules for new learnings online approved by the Government and mandated by the World health organization and other health agencies under the Federal laws.

Continue reading…………………….

But time is going to heal soon with the world's new situation and you are going back to physical school, you're going to see crush in the same school that you didn't expected, taking up the same course and you became classmates…. :-)

But of course, you're focus on your studies, and just make crush as your motivation to strive hard.

Then he approached you and ask for what's the homework, but you didn't know that he's noticing you slowly and surely, but for you it is too awkward and you feel so shy…

But nope, you'll going to stick to your plan to finish college.

All day every day you're in school, listening and participating to class.

Some other days will be a sort of schools founding Celebrations or the Foundation Day and that's going to be once a year, some are P.E. Day, and more programs depends on the University College you're at.

Some are just ordinary days with all pure lectures.

Then you go to your apartment or any rent place you have, fix your things, do homework, studying, and some sort of writings, doing your laundry on your own, cook for your own, sleep, then go to class the next day and so on and so forth.

You've learned every single bit of life and struggles by living on your own.

In preparation for your journey looking for a better job after you Graduate.

Finally, the day of your Graduation came, and you're so excited to receive your diploma.

That day of your Graduation, when you're wearing your toga and your graduation cap, someone approaches you to say Congratulations, not expecting that it is your crush…. :-)

Your parents are looking at you with pride and gladness, and thankful to the Lord that after all them

sacrifices, you made them fulfill what they wanted in life for you.

You're now ready to face the world, but learning never stops even after you finished college.

Learning is never ending.

Learning is a day to day in life basis so you could grow every day in every step of the way.

Then your crush is one of the reasons why you made it because he inspires you.

Until you met him on the same workplace.

He courted you and you connect each other's heart.

Dream Came True. :-)

End

Until then…… see you on my next book! :-)

faithstephenscopyrightsreserved2020

Your Inspiration

By: Faith Stephens

WORLD'S #1 READER FRIENDLY AUTHOR

Your Inspiration

About the Author: I want to share my insights to all the new generations of today of how to value life, making progress in our daily life routine. I love to teach values and share what I've learned throughout my existence. I am one of those authors who wants to make the world a better place.

Faith Stephens

Introduction:

People tend to have their inspiration in life.

It is very substantial to have an inspiration. Life is a complex matter of continual change.

We sometimes don't understand what's our purpose in life. Now, in order for you to have a purpose, you must to see around you of what you have.

Either family, friends, close companions, your own children, your siblings, and anything that is a part and important to your life.

You may find yourself wanting of a thing, a material thing.

The kids of today always wants to have devices like gadgets, new toys, new bags and shoes, new bikes and sometimes even food.

Continue reading…………………………

Teenagers always wants to have mobile devices, laptops, headphones, cute notebooks, and sometimes accessories like hair accessories, mobile accessories, and body accessories like a watch or a pair of earrings, and some sort of writing materials which they find cute.

Adults are all so into food and shoes, bags of course.

We all through all of the material things, but what I'm talking about is we need inspiration which can be felt and not just only can be seen.

Perhaps, you have the love of your life, your Mom, Your Dad, or your siblings.

Or perhaps your one and only true love.

People are people, they feel loved, they want to be loved.

We humans are specially uniquely designed to express our feelings.

Feelings somehow can't be touched; it can only be felt.

Sometimes the severity or the level of feelings depends on the individual or the person's experiences in life.

Many of us go to any other places, which we can explore and develop how to learn, somewhat a matter of making memories either alone or with somebody else in our life.

It is essential that we feel everything that surrounds us.

We feel the cool air, the wind breeze from the ocean when we're on a beach vacation.

We can taste the sweetness of sugar on our tropical pineapple juice, we can smell the good smell of rose petals in the garden of colorful flowers.

Continue reading………………………………………

God design us by the will of his own power. We are genuinely uniquely created by His love and greatness.

Each one of us have our own different way of expressing our feelings.

People are always amazing in a way that they can create a beautiful outcome out of their feelings.

Once we're inspired, we can do things unexpectedly and turn these things into productive matters like materials or even through writings.

Once a person is inspired, he or she can create a good song, a good rhythm and a good beat on tune.

A person that is inspired can beat the world.

It is always good to seek an amazing field into your life.

We all have our different characteristics and way of releasing our happiness into such way that we're also lifting ourselves into a better way.

Continue reading…………………………………

It shouldn't be always constant; it should always be moving. It should always be improving.

While we are in school, while studying, unaware that we're developing our skills, our intelligence our

knowledge way upgrading into something dynamic something spectacularly awesome.

It's all a state of mind, depends on the way your mind's processing those info …
Once you train your mind positively, you'll not going to end up regretting or to be hopeless.
Positivity can help people into many ways, it is always good to think positive.

Lower expectations than expecting a perfect life … because life is a matter of ups and downs.

As humans we sometimes can feel the loneliest times which can sometimes be that long, even longer for a year… but when you are brave and you know to yourself that you can do it, you can make it, you'll always become the happiest person on earth than those who see life on the negative side.

People needs their inspiration, they need someone to love, someone to hold, someone to kiss, someone to cuddle, and it makes them happy and complete.

It's the chemical substances in the body called dopamine and endorphins that travels into the brain which helps human like us feel that way.

We need someone to be with in our life until we get old.

Continue reading…………………………………………….

Just make sure you and your partner have the same interest in life. You view life as one, you have the same likes, maybe not much of the dislikes, but you enjoy each other's company.

The laughter and sharing of one's values are very important.

Talking something happy with your beloved makes the world goes round.

It feels like the time never stops, never ends, and never has numbers on it.

The joy with the one whom you're very compatible with is very priceless.

Never in the world that you can find a person like that but he or she is so extraordinary for you.

If you already have that person, don't waste time, don't miss the chance to make that person feel he/she Is really important and that you're making your time with her/him valuable and unforgettable.

It's just rare that couples knew what to just before doing certain things to make their loved one happy and makes time worth spending for.

I love how God created us special in a way that we feel, we love, we appreciate even small things, we can reason it all out, we can speak freely and do good.

Continue reading…………………………………………………….

When you choose love, doesn't matter how much the person earn, doesn't matter of the person's looks, doesn't matter how they're doing with their life.

Age never really a big deal when you choose love.

The physical looks, yes to some people, that really matters to them, but in my own personal view that's more of a person's pride.

When you love deeply, you feel the connection with you both…even if you don't speak too often with each other…even when you don't see each other that much.

Many people look for inspiration to be able to strive hard, and or to strive even harder to life.

Yes, that's a basic daily list, to find your inspiration.

Making life worth to live.

After all it's not all about money matters.

We mature, we learn day by day, we get older every year, we fail, we succeed, we let our guards down, and sometimes things around us things in our lives fall apart…but even though things get tough, we get up from our downfalls, we try to see things on the different side and make it even better.

If we need to look back into our past experiences, that would do, to think over and compare that the best of our lives is ahead of us…

God has His own plan for the best of us all.

We should think clearly, we should think of improvements and success.

Learn to appreciate life and love your life.

Sometimes to start for a positive vision in life will start into yourself.

Things will only work when you keep moving.

Learning how to love is one way of keeping yourself inspired.

We need to reach out to our true friends in times of there's much in need of confidants.

We need family, because it is said that family knows best for us.

We need to hold on into our special someone if we really and truly love them.

Despite what life brings to us, be confident!

Life will really teach us everything in this world. Life has lots to offer.

Choose the people whom you are going to be happy with when around.

Explore what you might want to explore to find yourself.

There are other times when it will take time for that, it will take time to find your soul… or to even find your soulmate.

Everything falls in the right place at the right time. All you need to have within you is patience, faith and hope.

Always put God first before anything else and you'll find your peace.

Hope you enjoyed reading... ☺

See you in my next book!

faithstephensCopyrightsreserved2020

How to choose the one you Marry

By: Faith Stephens

World's #1 reader friendly Author

How to Choose the One You Marry

Pure Love.

(Interesting Ways to Show to Your Partner)

Couples these days differ from couples from the past generations. They differ from the way they dressed. They differ from the way they talk, danced, and act. More of the millennials of today are so into the idea of playing video games, and chatting online instead of talking in person.

It is really so important to value and treasure the old days, for the reason that they know how to value a person very well, they know how to talk smoothly, nicely and gently, they know how to value time and how to respect each other's way and perspective in life.

Many young couples of todays are dealing with the scarcity of daily living, and because of that there are few who stand still and others have to let go. Well, perhaps that's the thing in life, of how to face the trials and consequences whenever it arises.

Take it from friends, grandparents, or even parents whom you know how they survived and you know that's been living still for so long at this very present moment, of how they face the storm together and not letting go of the hand.

Continue Reading……………

Love has different sides. Every person has their different point of views, different values, culture of what they believed in, and of different aspects in life.

First, is you got to learn these things within yourself… because in that way, you will know and understand human nature, human feelings, and instincts, and of course of how you value life, and that involves family, friends, coworkers, classmates, and the one that is really so dear to you the one you love.

Continue reading……………

We meet a lot of people in our lives …

We meet different cultures, religions, and tribes…

But we all do exist for one thing … and that is to love …

Continue reading…………………

Doesn't matter what color, doesn't matter what dialect, doesn't matter what country you came from, but what we all need to do, is to value one another because we all are living our life.

Now, in choosing the perfect partner in life, he /she should be observant in a right way and of the right things…

You need to know that person more …. You need to be friends first for a long period of time, to know if that person is really worth your trust and to be devoted with for the longest period of time.

But first you should know of ways of how to live in a peace and harmonious way of life. …. So that when problem arise, you can handle all of the test of time that will come your way.

Being in a relationship should be like a solid rock. You need to be tough, you need to be emotionally, physically, mentally, and maturely prepared.

It's all in yourself whom you can really rely on at first before allowing yourself to get involved with a new person in your life.

You need to learn that everything in this world doesn't come in easy form, doesn't come as easy as you wish it is … but you need to teach yourself how to become a better person first, and then whenever it is time to you to get out of your shell, then you can face all tough lucks ahead of the way because you're ready.

Continue reading…………………………

It all comes with experiences…. Yes, and experiences comes in all forms… while you're driving a car, that is already called experience. As you go along the road, you meet different traffic situations, and you need to observe traffic signs and traffic rules

, because if you're pretty much not paying attention then you will be given tickets for your traffic violations and you wouldn't want that because it's not easy to earn a hard-earned money out from your sweat working in a tough job and then you just need to spend the money just to pay a ticket disobeying the traffic rules… of course you wouldn't want to do that repeatedly in everyday so you'd be cautious, take precautions, and got to be careful around.

Continue reading……………………………….

You don't need to worry if they break your trust, all you have to think about is that you know it to yourself that you can live life even if without someone. That starts the courage within you, within the inner aspect of the stronger you.

Your life doesn't depend onto someone else, into somebody else, who doesn't see the same as what you think of yourself that you can….and you don't have to waste your energy to make them convince, but just prove them you can and show them the outcome and great success you have in life.

Every good thing is earned, respect is earned, and every success should start within yourself.

Continue reading………………………

People who are really down before are those who are successful now.

It is more likely comparable into a relationship you won't let the wrong past to experience ever again. That's why you need to see if the person you would want to be with for the rest of your life is with the same goal like you do.

It is unlikely to find such kind heart which is not only superficial.

You know when it is not just superficial is when that person gave up everything in life just to stay and live with you for good.

Ups and downs all the trials would come that's for sure, but a really serious deep feelings won't easily give up, just don't take further actions to mess things up and avoid issues and negative confrontations and conversations…. that wouldn't help settle things up.

Continue reading………………………

If you truly love someone, you have to correct that person's mistake in a very calm loving approach.

There are too many problems in the world, which we don't want to add up to those problems right?

Same as in dealing with our relationship, every each of us has our bad side and good side…. but we would want to stay and focus in the good side for a better and meaningful life and a good and harmonious relationship with each other.

Continue reading…………………….

To rush things is of no good… to rush things out would lead you into a wrong way, a wrong destination of your life… there's always a saying that you need to wait for the right time, in God's perfect timing.

To know someone is not that easy, it isn't just a snap…

You got to be sure if you have the same likes, or the same goals in life.

If you and that person listens to the same music, or of having the same interest to listen to different kind

of music, or if that person whom you would love to be with prefers to watch television instead of music.

If of course that person would cook for you, or in reverse you would cook for her/him.

Sometimes, each one of us have our own body scents, our natural body scents.

Some may have an unpleasant body scent or that's what they called a body odor.

When you live together, you got to deal with his/her natural body scents whenever he sweat from a very long day of work, or from the gym, or playing tennis or golf.

Then you should be ready to deal with the soiled clothes and socks in the hamper and do laundry later to clean them up.

Continue reading………………………

Not just that, but of course there are a lot of things to master such as cooking, watering the plants, planting some veggies in your backyard, cleaning your entire house.

If you see that your partner is capable of those things mentioned, then maybe that person is the right one for you.

Continue reading………………………

For some instance, it really depends on some people's own preferences.

Some of them prefers, beauty before capabilities.

Some of them prefers talent before beauty.

Continue reading…………………….

Some of them prefers education before beauty, because they think this way "what's there with their beauty if that person is not smart enough to think what to do in daily life occurrence especially when problems arises when they aren't have the ability to plan before taking actions."

Whenever it is , or whatever their reasons could possibly be, but we should respect each of their preference, if that will make them happy, because all of that is for them that maybe they could handle well.

Life's too short not to find your happiness.

We should be eager to find what makes us happy. Let go of things that weights you down.

Find your best self within you first.

Continue reading………………………

Others may have taken their strengths from their past experiences to make them stronger, even stronger to fight life's battle.

They are able to manage their ups and downs because they develop self-trust , self-discipline and self-worth when the time they were alone.

They are really admired because they became successful and have reached their goals in life through wealth and education.

Some may just have wealth but still they are awesome with their good hearts.

They share their blessings through giving and reaching out to those people who need their help...

but on the other hand, there are people who doesn't do same, but all we have to do is teach them the good way, and lead them to the bright side of their future.

This is just the same when you're in a relationship, you need to go hand in hand in life together, help each other throughout your life.

It is never easy, and will going to be rough when kids come all the way through.

Continue reading...........................

Everybody else faces problems in their relationship.

It is really challenging when this arises because through this you will know how strong you are, and you will both know how strong you both are.

Whenever there are misunderstandings, both should talk, and express what they feel.

If you feel upset at a certain reason, you need to let your behalf know, so you can clear things out.

Things, money, and pride are only superficial. You cannot even take these when it is time for you to take the path of the afterlife.

We cannot be boastful because we want to win the argument or we cannot be too selfish because you cannot swallow your own pride.

Sometimes the very nice feeling is to be kind and gentle and let the universe shower your bountiful joy which comes from a natural occurrence or a surprise gift of love from God above.

Have you ever experienced the time when you feel empty, when you feel down deep inside and you couldn't figure out for solutions, but when you pray and when you let God lead the way, help comes all naturally?

That's when you not let sadness take over your emotions and the inner you.

It's you whom you know to yourself what's bad and good for you.

Continue reading……………………………….

Inspire yourself to the wonders of the world, and make your dreams a reality.

Somehow, and sometimes in our lives, we find that person who is willing to go to our journey.

You wouldn't know if you found that person already unless if you try to take a look carefully and feel the aura of their soul who makes you laugh, who makes you smile the whole time, who helped you whenever your down, and who is eager to be with you for the entire generation.

Continue reading ………………………….

If everything's cannot be solved by talks, then talk to that person again, just don't give up no matter how many times you need to talk with the person you love.

You can be super extra sweet if you needed to, give chocolates, flowers and cards if you needed to.

You can give perfumes, Order food, gift cards or what you may think for that person's favorites.

Try to analyze the situation too. If it is too much of a quarrel or argumentation, you would know.

Too much is not good too. You can say no if you needed to. You can stay and continue if you wanted to if that really defies your love to that someone you love.

Continue reading………………………….

Trust, Love, Hope and Faith are the spices of love.

It may involve deeper understanding too, because without understanding, you and your partner would not go that far.

So, first you really have to love yourself. Accept yourself of who you really are.

You need to settle things out first in yourself, you have to educate yourself and be open to the different side of the world, to each person's differences, to each people's culture.

One would say that a happy person will always be happy and contented.

Being in a relationship is not that easy of what you think it is, so as being married.

There are couples who parted their lives not being able to survive together because of their individual differences and we don't want to end into that part because we need a life companion, we need a lifetime partner who will support for us and who will take care of us when we get old and gray.

Continue reading…………………………….

We need someone whom we can talk to by the end of the day, who will ask us how's our day have been.

All we need in this world is love, take care of your partner and be happy ▢

See you in my next book.

@FaithStephensCopyrightSeriesOf2021